Technology is Accelerating can Education Catch Up?

NORMAN HALLS

It dedicated to all those who are involved in industry-education partnerships that have confidence in the future workforce in what the United States needs to stop the erosion of manufacturing technology. "While these impending changes hold great promise for future prosperity and job creation, many of them also pose major challenges requiring proactive adaptation by corporations, governments, societies and individuals." WEF

Dedicate this to my loving family.

Contents

Educators face enormous challenges learning methodological innovation.

Parents and teachers are motivators for children in identifying their interests.

Classroom aligning technology is a powerful support tool.

We build relationships, problem-solve, and be creative thinking.

Educators will have to change their current preparation.

Requirements for certification should include academic subjects and terminology from the industry.

There are several partnerships that educators and industry can get involved.

Introduction

Global competition, U.S. education(K-12) while essential skill development and workforce preparation skills are crucial to the American education system. The paradigm shift must take place, recognizing that to be indeed globally competitive, and we must be globally competent. If America is to maintain a seat at the table, we must prepare our students to bring competitive skills to this new world market. We've heard this cry for globally competitive skills so often now it has become trite. It's time for action to replace words. There is a significant company's involvement with school systems providing support for the Four Industrial Revolution terminology. Local businesses will get the benefits from them, but home-grown involvement profits from future workforces.

If Americans are to continue to prosper and to exercise leadership in this new global context, it is imperative that we understand the new global forces that we have both shaped and had thrust upon us. The alternative is to be at their mercy. — Edward Fiske

With the changing technology future workforces are going to have to adapt at greater haste than years pass. The risks are tactical, affecting an organization's ability to expand capacity, grow revenue, increase productivity, and reach higher profitability. It will be a shared responsibility to seize opportunities and find solutions. Educators must change their method of teaching to incorporate terminology for the 21st Century. A. Rotherham & D. Willingham wrote: "If these skills were indeed new, then perhaps we would need a radical overhaul of how we think about content and curriculum. But if the issue is, instead, that schools must be more deliberate about teaching critical thinking, collaboration, and problem-solving to

1

all students, then the remedies are more obvious, although still intensely challenging." Willard R. Daggett wrote: "If the American education system is to prepare its students to meet the demands of an increasingly technological world, indeed if it is to be effective at all, it must integrate technology into the academic curriculum. The prospect of personal technology in school, however, makes some teachers and administrators uncertain about how to proceed. After all, what will students be doing with their cell phones and personal digital assistants (PDAs)? Will they be looking up facts on the Internet, seeking answers from friends, or perhaps sending a copy of a test to a friend?" Unfortunately, all indications are that the United States has some distance to go in preparing students for the Fourth Industrial Revolution. Current data show that U.S. students seem to be less prepared than their foreign contemporaries.

As we embark on the Fourth Industrial Revolution, it's clear that technology will play a central role in nearly all aspects of our lives. Research by the World Economic Forum estimates that 65% of children entering primary school will find themselves in occupations that today do not exist. Will schooled radical overhaul and required curriculum change needed with industry in the 21st Century? Will educators have the background to teach the terminology necessary in the 21st Century? How can schools move at the same fast-growing pace as the industry? How much workforce experience should they have in the classroom? Dennis Frezzo said: "While experts believe that the human psychology behind learning has not changed vastly over time, the external factors affecting how we comprehend, retain and receive new material are constantly evolving. As the digital revolution accelerates, technology gives us exciting opportunities to shape learning experiences and achieve learning goals." Gloria Latham, The University of Sydney, wrote: "Should teachers

2

have 21st-century mindsets, be lifelong learners, adventurous, innovative and imaginative? Should they be individuals who were outsiders to traditional systems of learning? Or, do we continue to value what teachers know over who they are? If we value who they are, how might we attract these vibrant role models to teach?"

World educational efforts to reformulate education for 21st-century teaching and learning are well-funded initiatives by alliances, including governments and large corporations. In Helsinki, Finland – BIAC reports: "Education is vital to productivity, employment, and growth in the 21st-   Century. The competitiveness of economies and companies hinges to a great extent on the talent of their people. Employers, therefore, have a profound interest in ensuring that today's and tomorrow's jobseekers are educated, employable, and can continue to learn throughout their lifetimes." If education does not introduce new content, but it enriches the concepts and materials of all subjects and fields of knowledge related to global development by widening their dimensions. All curriculum(K-12) should include terminology required for better-skilled workers

U.S. competitiveness and the country's standing among our global counterparts have been persistent issues in public policy debates for the past 20 years. Most recently, they have come to prominence with the publication of reports argues that the United States is in danger of losing out in the economic competition of the 21st Century.

  Unless the United States maintains its edge in innovation, which found in a well-trained creative workforce, the best jobs may soon be overseas. If current trends continue, along with a lack of action, today's children may grow up with a lower standard of living than their parents. Providing high-quality jobs for hard-working Americans must be our

3

priority. Indeed, it should be the central goal of any policy in Congress to advance U.S. competitiveness.

The United States is in direct competition with countries that recognize the importance of developing their human resources. The numbers and quality of scientists and engineers educated elsewhere, notably in China and India, continue to increase, access to scientific and engineering talent possible wherever it exists. The result is that U.S. scientists and engineers must compete against their counterparts in other countries, where living standards and wages are often well below those of the United States. Policies for maintaining U.S. competitiveness must consider how to ensure that employees are educated to have the skills and abilities that will be in demand by industry. Because the foundation for future success is a well-educated workforce, the necessary first step in any competitiveness agenda is to improve science and mathematics education.

In an ever-changing, increasingly complex world, it's more important than ever that our nation's youth are prepared to bring knowledge and skills to solve problems about artificial intelligence (AI). Diversification is necessary for education and industry to continue to thrive in the future. The realization of educators to have the curriculum must include a growth mindset for 21st-century terminology for the community to prosper and the students to have the means to advance into the workplace.

"So, what should we tell our children? That to stay ahead, you need to focus on your ability to continuously adapt, engage with others in that process, and most importantly retain your core sense of identity and values. For students, it's not just about acquiring knowledge, but about how to learn. For the rest of us, we should remember that intellectual complacency is not our friend and that learning – not just new things but new ways of thinking – is a life-long endeavor." Blair Sheppard, Global Leader

Chapter I Mindset

There has been a reluctance by educators to make any changes to a curriculum. A program was presented to a high school clerical class in 1970. The plan was to introduce Word Processing on a system by Xerox Alto. Xerox was donating the computer, and the state department of education had approved for a grant. But first, it had to have the school department and the high school to support. The clerical chairperson read the grant proposal, and her comment was: "I have taught this course for 30 years; I'm not changing it." The students lost years of exposer to the new innovative clerical method.

Resentment, among educators against the using high technology terminology in schools had been significant, such as: "Around here high tech is a nasty word" (a science department chair); "I have a terrible hatred for high tech," (a mathematics department chair); and "I won't sit in the same room with those people" (an assistant superintendent said). Educators firmly believe that the traditional method of instruction is the best. Hence, there is a need to change the mindsets of educators towards use for technology in classrooms to meet the current demands of learners.

Advances in information and communication technology are reshaping the ways educators convey learning experiences to learners. Consequently, educators need to acquire and utilize the necessary information and communication technologies of today. William Tolley, Education Week wrote: What does this mean for our work? Teachers committed to creating 21st-century learning environments must rely on the same growth mindsets we seek to cultivate in our students. We must be committed to inventive interpretation and growth in practice as we push on in the face of outdated notions of what "teaching" looks and sounds.

The term "21st-century learning" has been used to refer to ability students must master, such as problem-solving skills, critical thinking skills, and digital literacy. Some refer to it as the ability to collaborate, communicate, and demonstrate skills that will ultimately help students navigate their way in the future. The idea of what 21st-century learning is open to interpretation and controversy. Today's educators need to use teaching strategies to equip students with the characteristics and skills that will help them live in this ever-changing technological world. The only way that we can do that is by having our 21st-century characteristics and abilities.

"Undertake something that is difficult, it will do you good. Unless you try to do something beyond what you have already mastered, you will never grow." — Ronald E. Osborn

However, it also to foster the ability to solve problems and take challenges, to prepared them to tackle issues they face outside of school. Decades of research have demonstrated that a student's mindset is a critical factor that impacts how comfortable and motivated they are when posed with a new or difficult problem to solve. Specifically, students who possess a growth mindset are more motivated to learn and take on more challenges compared to students with fixed mindsets (Blackwell, Trzesniewski, & Dweck, 2007). Given this research, many educators have been incorporating growth mindset strategies into their interactions with students in their classrooms for several years. Despite the growing use of educational technology in the classroom, there has been little focus on the role of these tools in shaping a student's approach to learning. This paper explores what it means to have a growth mindset and how supporting this perspective in students can be enhanced in the context of educational technology." Wrote Elizabeth Kazakoff and Alison Mitchell

Growth mindset research is on the rise among scholars of teaching and learning because of its perceived ability to impact student engagement and outcomes. Developing a growth mindset is as equally applicable to staff and teacher performance as it is to students. Keith Heggart commented; The crucial point for individuals is that these mindsets have a significant impact upon our understanding of success and failure. A fixed mindset people dread failure, reflects poorly upon themselves as individuals, while growth mindset people instead embrace failure as an opportunity to learn and improve their abilities.

Chapter II Growth Mindset: Change in Thinking

Business/employers must change their thinking to compete in today's industrial revolution. The fourth industrial revolution is here; those that support human creativity are the front-runners. "When we understand how people think and work best, we will be compelled to put our workers' well-being first in the name of both health and economic productivity." By Itai Palti.   As you approach the industrial revolution challenge, you have to have talent. Talent with a growth mindset, you need to upgrade up your strategies and determination, physically, and expand your abilities. Take the growth mindset action. You need to recognize that a growth mindset is not just superiority but supported by knowledge. In other words, you need to be committed to developing a growth mindset. Research shows that people who feel in control tend to perform better. "Growth mindset companies can also feel more inclusive because employees are more willing to collaborate." Harvard Business Review Staff, 2014.

The growth of mindset can increase an organization, focusing on people's capacity. As such, recruitment should value people who show a real commitment to learning a new strategy. These people will help build a process, develop independently, collaborate successfully, and be more able to adapt to whatever challenges arise. Individuals that value learning, and show a capacity and passion for continual knowledge have a natural growth mindset that can move any business towards success.

Developing new products, a process, companies need to sufficiently define the problems they're attempting to solve and clearly expressing why those issues are essential. "Without that the firmness, organizations miss opportunities, misuse resources, and end up pursuing innovation initiatives that aren't associated with their strategies. How many times have you seen a project go down one course only to realize in retrospection that it should have gone down another? An innovation programs

conveys a seemingly breakthrough result only to find that it can't implement or it addresses the wrong problem? Many organizations need to become better at asking the right questions so that they tackle the right problems." Dwayne Spradlin Harvard Business Review.

"What we found most critical are two things: a "collaborative mindset" and learning how to collaborate successfully. One of our assessment tools (TCEP), is a metric of how collaborative a team or organization is. This metric is subjective, but it does allow everyone to put themselves on the same scale, so comparisons of groups, teams, and departments, can happen. We worked with several different teams at General Dynamics and found that each team's effectiveness was different. We found that teams where the collaboration was smoother, often had better performance (i.e. completing tasks more quickly, and higher quality output). Although there was no clear way to measure this, working with other organizations found that teams that collaborate well are often are 20-25% more productive than teams that don't. So, it is worthwhile to help teams adopt a collaborative mindset as it can affect the bottom line!" by Collaborative Strategies, Inc.

Employers and their employees "who believe their talents can be developed (through hard work, good strategies, and input from others) have a growth mindset. They tend to achieve more than those with a more fixed mindset." A. Nguyen at Harvard. Employees with a growth mindset view talent and intelligence as a starting point, and they then focus on improving their capabilities. A mindset is a set of assumptions, methods, and ideas held by an individual or exercised by a group. In practice, mindsets are everywhere around us. Evidenced by people's adoption and acceptance of certain behaviors or choices that already established; most often, these mindsets referred to as rules or conventions. Concerning the innovation equation, mindsets can be very good or very bad established norms — it just depends on what is involved in each set.

Companies need to stop and go back to basics and CEOs, and their Senior Management teams need to set a vision for the company, so everyone knows where they are, where they want to get to, and what values underpin this vision. They champion corporate profits, and all employees buy into it for success to occur. It helps achieve a 'growth mindset' by empowering employees and ensuring that they are all on the same page.

Chapter III Industry Education K-12 in Other Countries

On the global stage, U.S. domination eroded the past decade, and China and India are projected to the U.S. in terms of economic output by 2050. "Why so little attention on education governance, then, if it is central to constructing a system of schooling that can meet the demands of the current century?" commented McGuinn and Manna. If the United States hopes to achieve the leading in the world in the technology revolution, educators must collaborate with all of the workforces. E. Lento, Ph.D., wrote: "Around the world, digital technologies are demonstrating their ability to empower educators in their mission of developing the next generation of lifelong learners, innovators, and global citizens. With an effective technology foundation and the right support, teachers gain powerful tools to deepen, accelerate, and enhance student learning."

The introduction of technology has revolutionized education, and that has given birth to new modes of education. One of the new modes that have changed the way education imparted is K-12 education. K-12 education is an educational concept that is widely gaining popularity in countries like the United States of America, Canada, and India as well, among other countries. This kind of educational system is different from the conventional method of teaching and involves a more teacher-student communication than the current version. Read on and find out more about the K-12 education system and its presence in India. The K-12 education system includes much teacher-student interaction with the teacher encouraging a lot of question-answer sessions, assignments that would promote new learning habits in students. Individual attention is another critical factor in the education system. This method of teaching is beneficial, and students develop are learning their capabilities on their own. The teacher plays the ideal guiding star in their success. One of the main points that sets this system apart from its conventional from typical classroom activity. Students

preparing and submitting assignments, and they are also encouraged to add values to their assignments in the form of personal views and ideas. They are also motivated to take part in various discussion clubs and forums to exchange ideas and views. (fedena)

There is a more major emphasis on problem-solving concepts. The consensus for this prediction occurred after the second-round survey at the 82.8% agreement level. Educators understand that the world is increasing in complexity and that technology is pervasive. Today, employees are often required to utilize both technology and higher-reasoning skills, such as solving problems. Teaching students problem-solving skills invaluable. There more emphasis on understanding and utilizing computer systems in design and processing fabrication (e.g., CNC machining, rapid prototyping, robotics, automation). The consensus for this prediction occurred after the second-round survey at the 77.2% agreement level. Even small businesses are utilizing the computer-based systems once reserved for only the largest corporations. Consequently, students must understand how to use these computer systems to be more employable. The trend of more companies using computer systems in design and processing fabrication will most likely continue because reliance on computers continues to increase in the future. Elements of information technology and communication systems studied. The consensus for these two predictions occurred after the second-round survey at the 77.1% and 71.5% levels of agreement, respectively. The technologies involved in these areas are advancing at a fast pace. As technology changes, educators must be prepared for the first master and then teach them new technology to students. Students should understand current technology to have an advantage in the work arena. (L. Scott Hansen)

When thinking of the field of Education, becoming a teacher is the most obvious form of an educational career. Even within teaching, the subject areas and age groups are so varied that a range of options exists. Several areas that should be applied for employment are the understanding of how the world of work overlaps and needs to include in the curriculum. United States' failure to educate its students leaves them unprepared to compete and threatens the country's ability to thrive in a global economy and maintain its leadership role.

Education is a trillion-dollar industry. Katie Puckett wrote: "Skills to help us manage the formidable tools at our disposal. We need to know how to interpret search results, critically assess the quality and veracity of information and make ethical judgments about how to use it, and we'll need to think creatively to come up with solutions to increasingly complex global problems." Learning outcome in the ever-changing technology in the Fourth Industrial Revolution a key role in meaningful education. Focusing on learning outcomes is essential to inform diagnosis and improve teaching processes and student learning. Learning outcomes has to increase in response to a range of K-12 education trends, challenges, and standard shifts.

In the future, work structure around projects, not processes. That's a significant trend in education too. "Active" or "problem-based" learning seeks to engage students' natural curiosity, rather than merely presenting them with information. "That's the big shift in the way we're teaching: we're starting to mix things up," says John Holm at SocioDesign. "Instead of just saying 'here's stuff to remember,' it says 'here's a problem to solve,' and the students get involved in that problem."

Chapter IV Careers in the Past and Now

Looking back 50 years ago. Manufacturing had several employees at various skill levels. The U.S. economy added 263,000 jobs in April 1970; the unemployment rate fell to 3.6%. The 1970's was noticeably sawed increase trend within the manufacturing sector towards automation. Before, a single operator would press a button and made sure the machine ran efficiently. Advances in technology allowed for "an operator" to run a series of devices proficiently. These advances had many positive benefits, such as safety. The automation also meant that fewer people were required to produce and reduced the number of hourly workers.

However, the 1970s saw a massive uptake by manufacturers of computer technologies to lift production efficiencies. CNC machines were starting to be in everyday use in machine shops in the 1970s, with manufacturers faced with shortages of skilled machinists. The introduction of CAD/CAM allowed further increases in design ability and less time needed and with more accuracy. Manufacturers claimed CAD/CAM was the most useful, most used, and most beneficial application of computer technology. However, the highest level of progress of computer application was in the areas of process control and, by the late 1970s, this technology was appearing everywhere. Computer-controlled processing had its most significant impact on the primary metals processing trades, and in processes where heat, speed, and dimensional control is critical.

Manufacturing in the United States is a vital sector. The United States is the world's second-largest manufacturer (after China) with a record high real output in Q1 2018 of $2.00 trillion (i.e., adjusted for inflation in 2009 Dollars) well above the 2007 peak before the Great Recession of $1.95 trillion. The Boston Consulting Group articulates: Since joining the World Trade Organization in 2001, China has emerged as the workshop of the world. China's factories now generate more real manufacturing value-added—$3.7 trillion in 2017—than the US, Germany, South Korea, and the UK combined. China's manufacturing power is also evident in the vast diversity of industries in which it is globally competitive. Several compelling advantages are likely to enable China's manufacturing sector to keep growing, succeeding in global markets. By diversifying into higher-value areas—even if access to specific export markets becomes difficult.

L. Rafael Reif, President of MIT, wrote: The remarkable progression of innovations that imbue machines with human and superhuman capabilities is generating significant uncertainty and deep anxiety about the future of work. Whether and how our current period of technological disruption differs from prior industrial epochs is a source of vigorous debate. However, there is no question that we face an urgent sense of collective concern about how to harness these technological innovations for social benefit.

The Fourth Industrial Revolution began as an initiative for the manufacturing sector, which was suffering from dwindling productivity. The scheme was initially a reaction to the global over-reliance on financial services sectors, which had grown exponentially over the last few decades. One initiative that determines labor productivity is technological change. Natalie Bishop wrote: "Technological change is a combination of invention—advances in knowledge—and innovation, which is putting that advance to use in a new product or service. This change must be fueled by multi-stakeholder support and governance along with new approaches to deliver training programs rapidly to millions of workers affected by the ongoing transformations." Responsible leadership is the prominence on managers to make ethical choices when it comes to the issues of profit vs. job losses, and other topics brought about by new technologies. Lifelong learning will be a requirement for all workers to their up-skilling and learning further information throughout their careers, especially when it comes to technical vision.

Manufacturing and service leaders and workers must visualize the possibilities of the future. The future jobs to visualize can help business leaders, workers, educators, and policymakers shape their vision and spark conversations around what needs to change to make this happen. Manufacturers need employees who are highly skilled in technology, data science, and engineering. The future of work is no longer just about filling today's open needs; it's about re-evaluating the work and the workforce of tomorrow. What comes to your mind when you think of manufacturing? What if we told you that in the manufacturing industry of the future, you might not be able to get a job if you can't run a robot? Workforce and employer were well-organized to provide a vision into the tremendous benefits to the productivity of workers and provide the insights needed to better direct people and realize cost savings.

Chapter V Visualizing the Future

We must visualize the possibilities of the future. The future jobs to visualize can help business leaders, workers, educators, and policymakers shape their vision and spark conversations around what needs to change to make this happen. Teresa Amabile and Mukti Khaire HBR wrote: "Creativity has always been at the heart of the business, but until now it hasn't been at the top of the management agenda." Creativity is essential to a business that gets a new start, and that sustains the best company after they have reached production. But perhaps because of its creation is considered unmanageable—too elusive and intangible to pin down—to produce a less immediate payoff is the focus of most managers' attention.

Perhaps it's no wonder the United States is facing a decline in new projects that manufactured when products that are made offshore and not here. "The United States of America—for generations known around the world as the land of opportunity and innovation—is on the verge of losing its competitive edge. It is facing perhaps its greatest economic challenge since the dawn of the industrial revolution. This challenge has little to do with business costs and even less with manufacturing prowess. And, no, the main competitive threats are not from China or India," commented Richard Florida HBR. "The research reveals a strength of opinion that confirms, in corporate America today; the purpose is being driven by the workforce and other stakeholders. Companies are not only responding, but understanding that a company's social values are a defining part of its brand and success," said Jerry MacCleary, chairman and CEO of Covestro LLC

Stakeholders have a unique understanding of informing CEOs where products manufactured for the company's social understanding before profit. The role of business is to create value for its shareholders, but in such a way that it also creates value for society, manifesting itself as a win-win proposition. But the attitude must change to keep employment and profit in the United States. For years financial exploitation has occurred by offshore companies. Education and industry have not kept up with the future visualized long term along with corporate America. "How can the manufacturing industry get ready for the future of work and prepare workers to work with robots and advanced technologies? What are the skills that will become must-haves in the workplace? What are the pathways for training and education to enable these skills? Finding potential solutions to close the manufacturing skills gap begins by exploring what's possible for future jobs." Deloitte.

For example, this is what employers are up against: "On June 2018, the Chinese e-commerce giant JD.com unveiled a fully automated storage and shipping facility in Shanghai. The factory outfitted with twenty industrial robots that can pick, pack, and transfer packages with no human presence or oversight. Without robots, it would take as many as 500 workers to staff this 40K square foot warehouse fully — instead, the factory requires only five technicians to service the machines and keep them working." CB insights.

From the conception of your business idea to the way you carry out everyday business tasks, creativity is essential and be deeply ingrained in your workplace culture. Address an unmet industry need and design your concept based on the perspectives of your target users. Embrace diversity and collaboration within your team, and occasionally break from the usual work routine with new workplace practices. Embrace diversity and collaboration within your organization, and sometimes cut from the usual work routine with new workplace practices. "When it comes to the future of work, many organizations are missing the point. Executives are creating a new future of work initiatives every day, but to what end? Many of these initiatives suffer from being too reactive. For instance, managers may feel pressure to reduce costs by what the company is doing with machine learning and AI, and it's a critical time for organizations to focus their efforts. Imagine the benefits of a future of work strategy aimed at generating more value and meaning for the customer, the workforce, and other partners, and higher earnings for the company over time." Jeff Schwartz, John Hagel III, Maggie Wooll, and Kelly Monahan MITSloan

"It is the business of the future to be dangerous," said philosopher and mathematician Alfred North Whitehead more than eight decades ago. In times of constant change, organizations, education, and industry, that do not adapt, that do not challenge the status quo, are in danger of irrelevancy — or worse, extinction.

Chapter VI Constant Change

In times of constant change, organizations, education, and industry, that do not adapt, that do not challenge the status quo, are in danger of irrelevancy — or worse, extinction. The future of the United States depends on several factors in new insights for competency with industry. The graduate, high school or higher education, was sponsored by the taxes paid by homeowner and business. Having that understanding, we can govern what instructed is relevant. The graduates are or will provide activities with the workers of the future. People need the right skills and training for jobs in today's rapidly evolving economy. But globalization and advances in technology have transformed the nation's economy, and today's professions require better-skilled workers and a longer-term approach to training.

The Institute for a Competitive Workforce is the education and workforce program of the U.S. Chamber of Commerce reported the following: Sustained economic success requires a competitive workforce. A competitive workforce is produced by an educational system that instills in workers the knowledge and skills necessary to compete in the global economy. The reality is that the United States suffers from a skill gap, a problem that is projected to worsen. The educational systems are not equipping students with the skills needed, and inadequate retraining is taking place to retool workers to transition from declining industries to future ones. The pending retirement of 78 million baby boomers only exacerbates the problem. But there is hope. The government and the business community increasingly recognize the significance of the problem. There are examples of programs that are working, and education will be a priority for the next president. The business community must be engaged in this issue, as education and the skills of the workforce will have a direct bearing on the ability of companies and the country to compete going forward. Business must be heard at both the state and local levels and must be directly involved in helping to solve the problems that exist. "We speak a great deal about 21st-century learners and the skills, knowledge, and understandings they require. We appear to talk less about the qualities of the teachers. Should teachers have 21st-century mindsets, be lifelong learners, adventurous, innovative, and imaginative? Should they be individuals who were outsiders to traditional systems of learning? Or, do we continue to value what teachers know over who they are? If we value who they are, how might we attract these vibrant role models to teach?" wrote Gloria Latham University of Sidney. There are several factors needed to make changes in an educational system to future job possibilities; faculty resistance, mandated test guidelines and instructional curriculum, and each State requirements for a teacher. While few would disagree that the ultimate goal is full integration of 21st-century skills into all classes and curriculum, the task is overwhelming. It is simply beyond the reach of most school organizations. "Almost all educators acknowledge that the field has deep problems, but their concern has not been about the issues raised. Critics lack selectivity, an imbalance between content and pedagogy, or the lack of value delivered. These differences aren't always recognized because the insider critiques often sound a lot like the external critiques. In reality, insiders are more concerned about the chaos in the field." commented Kate Walsh EducationNext.

"The 21st-Century has seen a significant shift in learning goals—formal education sectors in countries all over the world want their young people to be able to think critically and creatively, solve complex problems, make evidence-based decisions, and work collaboratively. The primary issue facing countries, then, is how to implement fully a 21st-century skills agenda that focuses on teaching, learning, and assessment that assisting with changing educational goals." Brookings Institution.

Education is vital to productivity, employment, and growth in the 21st Century. The competitiveness of economies and companies hinges to a great extent on the talent of their people. Employers, therefore, have a profound interest in ensuring that today's and tomorrow's jobseekers are educated, employable, and can continue to learn throughout their lifetimes. First, let's consider what hasn't changed. Employers need to interact with educators to understand what their curriculum needs to emphases. Combine groups, collaborations with industry should link to a redefinition of the role of the educator in the 21st-century. Employers today still demand employees who can solve problems, collaborate, communicate, and be responsible for directing and assessing their performance. What has changed is that the need has become increasingly urgent. Challenges educators today is, 'How do we prepare today's learners for jobs that don't yet exist and which will require proficiency in technologies not invented? We define the specific knowledge or skills necessary to succeed in a global economy; it is imperative to equip today's learners with the required competencies to adapt and thrive. There is a growing recognition that traditional education, while just as critical to the intellectual development of our children, does not adequately address these needs.

Chapter VII Importance of Industry-Education Partnerships

The concept of Industry-Education Cooperation, Cooperative Education, and Internship has been a procedure for many years. There are three forms of industry alliances, Internship – really came in the 1980s, Cooperative Education – Herman Schneider at Lehigh University in 1901 devised the framework for the program, and Industry-Education Cooperation 1970 came together to form viable and vital partnerships with the stakeholders--industry (business, labor, government, and the professions) and education (public and postsecondary).

Three different programs with the same objects, students understand how their education relates to the world of work in the 21st century. Peter Serdyukov, Journal of Research in Innovative Teaching & Learning, wrote: "US education badly needs effective innovations of scale to produce the needed high-quality outcomes across the system. The primary focus of educational innovations should be on teaching and learning theory and practice, as well as on the learner, parents, community, society, and its culture. Technology applications need a solid theoretical foundation based on purposeful, systemic research, and sound pedagogy. One of the critical areas of research and innovation can be cost and time efficiency of the learning."

As three essential parts of society, education (K-12), university and industry sectors respectively take up important missions for social development and progress. Education and industry have been collaborating for over a century, but the rise of a global knowledge economy has intensified the need for strategic partnerships that go beyond the traditional pattern of discrete projects. Bold, visionary alliances between industry and education can accelerate innovation and help deliver solutions to pressing social challenges. Connect, collaborations with industry should link to a redefinition of the role of education in the 21st century. That role now extends beyond technology transfer to tackling critical social challenges and helping drive economic growth together. A new vision should include producing a highly skilled workforce for a knowledge-based economy. The education-industry partnership in the 21st century should be viewed not just as a generator of innovations but also as a channel of knowledge and competence that can effectively benefit society.

Models of industry-education started in 1970. Dr. Donald Clark in Buffalo, NY, developed a format for communities to adopt. The industry spends a considerable amount of time in Workshops, Classrooms, with school department personnel, conferences, and funding programs. Provide greater access to educational content, integrate physical and digital worlds for more engaging experiences, and improve decision making.

Industry and university collaboration dates back to the 1970s, and since 1973. The National Science Foundation's (NSF) Industry-University Cooperative Research Centers Program (IUCRC) facilitated partnerships among researchers from both industry and academia to drive innovation. Companies are hungry for ideas, and the actual technologies and intellectual properties to commercialize those ideas. And, companies are hungry for talent. "This is an excellent opportunity to expose students to the industry culture," Dorn Carranza says. "When students graduate, they are better prepared to start working at these companies." "Students trained in highly skilled industrial applications, are impacting the economy by creating a workforce that is relevant to those areas of national interest and industrial interest," Carranza says.

Chapter VIII How Students Benefit from Industry Education Cooperation

Michele Molnar Associate Editor Chicago wrote: Businesses, nonprofits, colleges, and community organizations are banding together with K-12 schools to form regional partnerships to help schools overcome technology challenges and promote innovation, team efforts that were highlighted here this week at a gathering of industry, education, and foundation leaders.

For education collaborators, the urgency to meet and learn from one another driven by students' needs, coupled with the ed-tech choices educators will be making over the next two years as their schools reach unprecedented levels of connectivity, said Richard Culatta, the director of the office of education technology at the U.S. Department of Education.

"We have to move fast." said Culatta

The risk of not coordinating efforts with K-12 schools, infusion of $8 billion to connect schools to broadband, students "will be in classes with high-speed Wi-Fi" and decisions on how to make the most of connectivity without data-driven research. Culatta urged organizations to act quickly to gather information about what works in terms of technology-based instruction, and get those findings to school decisionmakers.

Not all of the discussion focused exclusively on improving K-12 systems through teachers' use of ed tech. Among the many other topics tackled during the meeting:

- How can local and state governments become partners in the work of education innovation?

- When is it time to put an end to an unproductive partnership in a collaborative group of partners?

26

- What kinds of research are necessary to verify the value of work done in these partnerships, and who will pay for it?

- How can diverse organizations fully understand one another, when each has its lexicon for the work it does?

In the 21st Century developing curriculum and instruction models for skills for large numbers of Americans in business and education leaders to build collaborations that leverage their combined knowledge of labor markets, skills, pedagogy, and students. This integration of vocation and employment-oriented goals in academic educational programs has termed the "new vocationalism" movement. New vocationalism creates a well-rounded education that is the demand for skilled employees.   The need for a knowledgeable and engaged citizenry by integrating the three missions of community colleges: university transfer education, vocational education, and developmental education.

Student industry engagement techniques are a vital part of improving a student's learning experience (Rodrigues, 2004). Smith et al. (2009) stated that students who engaged with industry during their coursework succeed in their careers after graduation. Professors and lecturers can include student engagement activities in their courses, along with their lectures to provide students with the best possible learning experience. The present study focused on reviewing student learning outcomes resulting from various teaching techniques used in multiple industry engagements. Some of the industry engagement activities examined in this study were active activities, and others were passive, as defined by the literature. This study focused on reviewing industry activities using a holistic approach. These activities represent those currently used in university curricula, and they must be evaluated to gain an understanding of their effect on student learning. (Caleb Burns & Dr. Shweta Chopra)

What should students learn for the 21st Century? We must acknowledge the notion that obsolete methods, approaches, and educational models are failing to prepare children for a technologically-driven global economy. Textbooks must be rephrased. "21st-century skills are tools that can be universally applied to enhance ways of thinking, learning, working, and living in the world. The skills include critical thinking/reasoning, creativity/creative thinking, problem-solving, metacognition, collaboration, communication, and global citizenship. 21st-century skills also include literacies such as reading literacy, writing literacy, numeracy, information literacy, ICT [information and communications technologies] digital literacy, communication, and can be described broadly as learning domains." Wrote Ramya Vivekanandan Brookings

Times have changed! Gone are the days when students used to go to designated classes only, for learning and studying from their tutors. Technology is growing at the speed of light. All industries, all businesses are experiencing significant transformations due to daily advancements in technologies. The education sector is no exception. In this changing era, students are more driven towards using a mobile phone for every purpose. Everything they can access on their fingertips. So why not make the most out of it? "The education industry can outgrow exponentially by embracing the latest technology. If we talk about students, they can save their time to visit a library for searching for books and content they want. Just one benefit; there are many other benefits of mobile technology in the education industry for both educators (tutors) and students." From SoluLab

As part of the foundation of its developmental work, the project Industrial and Commercial Perspectives in Initial Teacher Education (ICP) surveyed existing industry-education work within initial teacher education. All institutions with BEd, PGCE, and concurrent courses were surveyed, using questionnaires directed towards educational studies and curriculum (methods) tutors. Respondents identified substantial benefits to students from involvement inactivity of this kind. The benefits were felt to include contributions towards greater maturity of outlook and an enhanced ability to relate to other adults, including parents of pupils. It considered that students gained more extensive knowledge of the outside world and broader perspectives on the aims and processes of education. A further view was that students were able to give their teaching greater reality and impact through the use of materials and examples and the involvement of people from industry and commerce. From Gordon Bloomer & Willian Scott British Journal of Education & Work

Chapter IX How Teachers are Involved with Industry

The emergence of these new relationships between education and industry has highlighted a need to examine and attempt to define teachers' work. The current debate has focused on the ability of teachers to make these links between education and industry. The education sector has put some effort into defining teachers' work in terms of knowledge, attributes, and skills required to be a teacher. For example, a project conducted in Australia by the National Project on the Quality of Teaching and Learning [NPQTL] has developed a set of National Competency Standards for Teachers. These competencies or skills imply a judgment of performance, that is, a way of measuring teachers' work.

These competencies are listed by NPQTL (1996) as:

> 1. using and developing professional knowledge and values;
>
> 2. communicating, interacting and working with students and others;
>
> 3. planning and managing the teaching and learning process;
>
> 4. monitoring and assessing student progress and learning outcomes; and
>
> 5. reflecting, evaluating and planning for continuous improvement.
>
> (Chris Perry & Ian Ball)

Industrial revolution 4.0 is a hot topic that in many economic, social, scientific, and technological forums. It is a revolution in smart manufacturing based on breakthrough achievements in the areas of artificial intelligence, virtual reality, mobile networks, the Internet of Things (IoT), cloud computing, 3D printing, biotechnology, nanotechnology, with the breakthrough of digital technology. In this new revolution (4.0), the concept of a virtual classroom, virtual teacher, the virtual device will become a trend in many schools in the coming time. What kind of teachers will continue to exist and develop in this revolution? Can tradition and technology coexist?

In the knowledge-based and digitized society of the 21st century, education faces the enormous challenge of transition from traditional learning to methodological innovation. It poses a unique demand for transforming teacher roles – the transmission of knowledge in a conventional way to the catalytic and coordinating role. In the digital age, the role of the teacher shifted from a mere point of view to the management of social behavior and emotion of the student, the mentor of learning to become a citizen of balanced development; Mechanical transmission for students with different degrees of speed in the digital environment.

The role of teachers in the XXI century becomes complex in a rapidly changing world; where knowledge is almost endless. Teachers must be technology-oriented and responsible not only for teaching but also for learning. They have to take into account the needs of each student in a heterogeneous classroom, creating a student-centered learning environment that enhances creativity, curiosity, and learning motivation.

To adapt to the 4.0 Industrial Revolution, students need to equipped with innovative capabilities, life-long learning, and access to digital technology. To successfully integrate and respond to future work, teachers must provide students with at least the following five skills (5Cs):

31

• Creativity: This is the most significant thinking scale in Benjamin Bloom's cognitive level (Bloom's Taxonomy Revised, 2002). Creative thinking will help students find solutions that are flexible, appropriate to the operating conditions that best serve the needs of the outside, and the needs of the individual.

• Collaboration Skills: This is an important skill in integration, students must know cooperation, human-human interaction, between human and intelligent machines with the goal of survival, play develop and achieve common goals.

• Communication: The ability to communicate and communicate in the digital age will be the key to enabling students to quickly access the knowledge store and interact with people to accomplish their goals.

• Critical thinking: It is the ability to analyze, understand, summarize and reflect on oneself to expand knowledge, improve thinking ability and adapt to the best.

• Continuous learning: Lifelong learning (learning to learn, learn to work and learn to live) will help students to be ready to receive and access new innovative as well as capacity of thinking of themselves.

Nam Ngo Thanh is now a manager of technology academy department in Ho Chi Minh City, Vietnam. Nam Ngo Thanh is now a manager of technology academy department in Ho Chi Minh City, Vietnam.

Chapter X How Parents and Teachers are Involved with Industry Education

In this era of stiff competition, selecting a decent career path has become very important for every individual. At times they get confused while deciding which career to choose. During such a situation, teachers and parents, in particular, play an essential role in identifying a child's skills and interests. They can provide proper guidance to students and can assist them in realizing their dreams.

Teachers and parents can act as motivators and can nurture the children. They can prepare them for a bright career and face challenges in the future. Inculcating certain important habits like reading and writing from an early stage can help them to get attuned to the competitive world. These days, it is complicated for parents to devote time to their children. As a result, they depend on teachers, schools, and coaching institutions for their child's education. (The Know Ledger View) Gallagher and Magid wrote, "children use devices like smartphones, tablets, Chromebooks, and laptops in school and the vocabulary full of technical jargon that seems completely foreign. One reason is that both tech-savvy and tech-hesitant parents are not always familiar with the world of education technology, or "edtech." The truth is that education technology is an essential part of education today, and parents should feel excited – not intimidated – by what their children can learn and do."

"Nearly one in four Americans is an enrolled student at any given time. This large segment of the U.S. population encompasses people of all ages and from all walks of life. American students have a wide range of educational goals—from learning their ABCs to obtaining an M.D.— to obtain the knowledge and skills they need.   Each of these students needs the support of dedicated educators. As a result of this great demand for talented educators, there are job opportunities for teachers in every geographical region of the country. Education is America's second-largest industry, and the different career tracks within education are as varied as the national population of its students." (AACC)

A teacher's goal is to advance their students' learning and cognitive abilities during the school year. For teachers today, looking toward the future can no longer focus on a single subject. He/she must have in their curriculum topics from different industries trends that assist students in having a look for the world of work. What should students learn for the 21st Century? We must acknowledge the notion that obsolete methods, approaches, and educational models are failing to prepare children for a technologically-driven global economy. Textbooks must be rephrased. "21st-century skills are tools that can be universally applied to enhance ways of thinking, learning, working, and living in the world. The skills include critical thinking/reasoning, creativity/creative thinking, problem-solving, metacognition, collaboration, communication, and global citizenship. 21st-century skills also include literacies such as reading literacy, writing literacy, numeracy, information literacy, ICT [information and communications technologies] digital literacy, communication, and can be described broadly as learning domains." Wrote Ramya Vivekanandan Brookings

School shops (industrial arts) classes may be a thing in the past. There ae substantial experiences in industrial arts education that impacts students' academic, social, and emotional outcomes. School districts are eliminating middle and high school shop classes for several reasons, but the bottom line, of course, is money. The American secondary educational system pumps as many of its competent students as possible into college. It seems that for some policymakers, 'academic' is a synonym for 'intelligent.' It is not. It has a much more limited meaning and refers to intellectual work that is mainly theoretical or scholarly rather than practical or applied. It is commonly used to describe arguments that are purely theoretical and people who are thought to be impractical. Of course, academic work is essential in schools, but human intelligence embraces much more than academic ability. This marvelous variety is evident in the extraordinary range of human achievements in the arts, sports, technology, business, engineering, and the host of other vocations to which people may devote their time and lives." wrote Ken Robinson Time Magazine. Vocational schools (also called career, technical, and trade schools) graduates on a path toward higher education in the 21st century, while the other-directed students towards jobs after they finished school. The definition of vocational: relating to an occupation or employment. Medical doctors, attorneys, professors, industrial and manufacturing, and science and technology are all vocations.

Chapter XI How Partnership Drives Innovation

Over the past decade, the business has changed dramatically. As a result, workforce skills and requirements have also changed. There are jobs today that didn't exist ten years ago. Such as data scientists, social media managers, and program developers, there will be new roles with new requirements that don't exist now. But while this has happened, one sector has lagged behind education, Said Michael King IBM.

Technology has an established track record and tremendous potential to transform learning and education institutions. Students can gain in learning programs that enrich their experiences and intervene when they struggle. Institutions can find better ways to allocate resources and operate more efficiently. Better outcomes, more productivity, what's not to like?

There are frequent arguments against more technology investment in education. Like any tool, technology can bring benefit or cause more problems than it solves. The positioned technology too much as driving productivity improvements in learning delivery, with Massive Open Online Courses (MOOCS) as the latest example, or we've used technology as a compliance and reporting tool, such as in K12 Education. One thing that might help change the discussion is shifting the focus to the instructor in the classroom and aligning technology as a powerful support tool. Teachers and faculty should have access to the same powerful tools offered to any other professional.

An example of this is the work IBM has underway with Memorial Sloan-Kettering to develop an advisor for oncologists using Watson, the self-learning computing system that won the Jeopardy! gameshow. The advanced system, combining natural language interface and self-learning algorithms, helps physicians create treatment plans. Similar tools could help teachers develop personalized plans to enrich student learning or intervene when they are struggling. We use a variety of advanced tools in support of patient care, from laboratory diagnostics to PET scans, but the physician is at the center of the process. The teaching profession deserves similar tools.

Putting teachers and faculty at the center of the process of learning is essential to driving student results. Online learning is growing by leaps and bounds, but ask yourself if you want your oncologist only to have an online learning experience as a credential. Classes and curriculum will transform by technology, and a lot of learning can be delivered online; there's a high value associated with on-premise, interactive work with others. Front line instructors should view as "assembly line workers," but as knowledge workers who play a critical role in advancing student learning. The biggest challenge we face in redesigning courses and curricular programs having the right activity in the correct sequence.

Too often, technology is seen as a compliance or reporting tool, with online tests and assessments as one example. These tools can be useful diagnostic tools for learning if delivered in timely, relevant ways. Again, finding the right mix to support those in the classroom to use technology effectively should be the focus. Shifting our focus to helping teachers and faculty as the front line of education can both change the investment priorities for institutions, as well as improve the dialogue around that investment.

Chapter XII Diversification and Growth Mindset

Very few companies ever get to the top or stay there, and the few that do remain there because they diversified. Immediate changes in competition demand are having a growth mindset. Consider what happened to Kodak. Their primary business income was not from cameras but from the film in which the photos developed. Kodak invented the first digital camera in the 1980s, but what did they do? They locked it up safely and told the engineer who designed it to keep quiet about it. Digital Equipment, a multimillion-dollar manufacturer of mainframe computers from the 1950s to the 1990s, missed out on personal computers. Ken Olsen, CEO of Digital Equipment, said: "The personal computer will fall flat on its face in business." Wang Laboratories' stumbling block was that their MS-DOS was not compatible with other systems. A generation of industrialists is erroneously being led to believe that they can succeed alone. But you need to plan and be ready to change. "If everything seems under control, you're just not going fast enough." Mario Andretti.

Carol Dweck, a Stanford University psychologist, "maintains that your mindset will play an important role in how you respond to feedback. Dweck distinguishes between people with a fixed mindset, who believe their intelligence and talent are fixed traits, and those with a growth mindset, who believe their basic abilities can be enhanced and improved through dedication and hard work. A person with a growth mindset will see constructive feed NOT as disapproval or criticism, but as an opportunity to learn how they can further improve and enhance their skills and performance".

A successful businessperson will likely tell you that the growth mindset is critical to your success in business. Professional people miscalculate how much mindset impacts all elements of their life, including business growth. "Definitions of mindset vary slightly depending on which source you refer too. Essentially mindset is the way you understand and respond to the world around you. It's about thinking, attitudes, beliefs, and behaviors and can influence everything from the way we build relationships, problem-solve, our creative thinking, how we perceive success and failure, valuing our worth and more" (Shevonne Joyce). A lot can determine our current mindset from what we prioritize and value.

Hewlett-Packard, at its foundation, calls for respect, integrity, teamwork, and innovation, among other core values. Reports: Tracy Keogh, Chief Human Resources Officer, HP. Building on the HP Way, we have defined practices and principles to guide employees as they go about their work. These will be shared early in the new year, helping to set expectations for how we work with each other when we're at our best.

Among these practices are a few that reinforce a growth mindset:

• Anticipate, learn, adapt: Don't become stagnant. The technology industry doesn't allow for complacency. Proactively seek what's next and understand what customers need, build your skills, be flexible, and resilient. In other words: Have a growth mindset.

• Make bold moves: Take informed risks, and dare to disrupt. It's the big ideas that help us make big leaps forward. When those bold moves are successful, great! When they're not, we want to be a company that shakes it off and asks, what did we learn?

• Connect, coach, empower: It's not just about having a growth mindset for yourself: it's about believing in the potential of your team and colleagues and helping them learn and succeed, too.

Chapter XIII Career Success Lack of Work Experience

A teacher's K-12 pathway is to college and teaching career lack of work experience.

Our founders recognized that public schools are a vital institution of American democracy. But education, they also knew, involved more than reading, writing, and arithmetic. Learning in a democratic society requires developing citizens who can adapt to changing times, make decisions about social issues, and adequately judge the performance of public officials. In fulfilling their responsibilities, public schools must not only provide knowledge of many subject areas and essential skills, but must also educate students on core American values such as fairness, equality, justice, respect for others, and the right to dissent.

Rapid social, political, and technological changes have escalated controversy over what and how schools should teach. Thus, educators frequently face a daunting task in balancing the educational needs of a diverse entire student body while maintaining respect for individual rights.

Where do teachers develop the knowledge and expertise for this type of instruction? The areas of undergraduate preparation, pre-service teacher education, and in-service professional development the primary influences, knowledge outcomes of three phases of teacher growth have been under-examined. To better understand how teachers, develop and deploy certain types of knowledge necessary for laboratory work, this paper addresses the following questions:

Q1. What kinds of teacher knowledge and skills are required to design and guide students through different forms of laboratory activity?

Q2. Do teachers' current preparation and professional development provide them with this knowledge and skills?

Q3. How should teachers' preparation and professional development be changed to foster the knowledge and skills necessary for effective laboratory instruction?

K-12 education is moving away from the traditional classroom model, where teachers lecture and students diligently take notes. Rather than sit in rows, today's students are more likely to sit in groups of three or four. This set up lends itself to collaboration and project-based learning, an approach to teaching in which students solve real-world problems using skills they will need for the future. These skills include things such as critical thinking, problem-solving, and communication.

In many instances, classroom technology drives this type of collaborative learning. A videoconferencing system might allow students to connect with other children around the world, exposing them to new cultures and new experiences without the cost of travel. An interactive display could enable multiple students to work on solving the same problem at once. Collaborative software and wireless presentation systems, like Apple TV, even allow teachers and students to share content from their mobile devices and display their screens for the classroom.

School systems across the country are encouraging partnerships between industry- education and other stakeholders, primarily, the private sector to enhance the performance of the education sector holds the key to unlocking the human resource development challenges. There is a good reason to believe that educational institutions must work proactively with industry, to deliver appropriately skilled and capacitated graduates to meet the societal and economic needs — the industry and education partnership initiative.

The speed of technological innovation and industry demands is moving faster in education's ability to adapt. The system

continues to focus on lectures and exams, leaving students underprepared to enter today's workforce. They're suffering as a result – along with businesses and higher education institutions themselves. How can we expect students to be productive and successful employees when we're using outdated models to prepare them?

Chapter XIV Changes by State Education Board Requirements

U.S. Department of Education - Technology offers the opportunity for teachers to become more collaborative and extend learning beyond the classroom. Educators can create learning communities composed of students; fellow educators in schools, museums, libraries, and after-school programs; experts in various disciplines around the world; members of community organizations; and families. This enhanced collaboration, enabled by technology offers access to instructional materials as well as the resources and tools to create, manage, and assess their quality and usefulness.

To enact this vision, schools need to support teachers in accessing needed technology and in learning how to use it effectively. Research indicates that teachers having an impact on students learning all school factors, business/industry responsibility to bringing technology-based learning experiences into schools. They need continuous, just-in-time support that includes professional development, mentors, and informal collaborations. The teacher requires more technology in their classrooms, and roughly half say that lack of training is one of the most significant barriers to incorporating technology into their teaching.

Institutions responsible for pre-service and in-service professional development for educators should focus explicitly on ensuring all educators are capable of selecting, evaluating, and using appropriate technologies and resources to create experiences that advance student engagement and learning. They also should pay special care to make certain that educators understand the privacy and security concerns associated with technology. This goal cannot achieve without incorporating technology-based learning into the programs themselves.

For many teacher preparation institutions, state offices of education, and school districts, the transition to technology-enabled preparation and professional development will entail rethinking instructional approaches and techniques, tools, and the skills and expertise of educators who teach in these programs. This rethinking should be based on a deep understanding of the roles and practices of educators in environments in which learning supported by technology.

We live in an age of relentless accelerations (McNeill & Engelke 2014). The combined forces of technology, globalization, and global warming are catalyzing changes in schools and societies wherever they may be found (Friedman 2016). Tectonic changes are reshaping U.S. workplaces as the economy moves deeper into the knowledge-focused age. These changes are affecting the very nature of jobs by rewarding social, communications and analytical skills. They are prodding many workers to think about lifetime commitments to retraining and upgrading their skills. And they may be prompting a society-wide reckoning about where those constantly evolving skills should be learned – and what the role of colleges should be.

We live in an age of relentless accelerations (McNeill & Engelke 2014). The combined forces of technology, globalization, and global warming are catalyzing changes in schools and societies wherever they may found (Friedman 2016). Tectonic shifts are reshaping U.S. workplaces as the economy moves deeper into the knowledge-focused age. These changes are affecting the very nature of jobs by rewarding social, communications, and analytical skills. They are prodding many workers to think about lifetime commitments to retraining and

upgrading their skills. And they may be prompting a society-wide reckoning about where those constantly evolving skills should learn – and what the role of colleges should be.

Pew Research survey finds that the vast majority of U.S. workers say that new skills and training will hold the key to their future job success.

The Pew Research analysis of jobs data in past decades, employment skills needed in jobs requiring higher levels of preparation, more education, training, and experience are required.

Educational change stands amid these transformations. Should schools abandon time-tested curricula in favor of teaching children computer coding, financial literacy, and group identity? Should schools encourage students to use Facebook, Twitter, and Snapchat as instructional tools–or should they forbid them because they serve as such seductive distractions from traditional and demanding disciplines like physics, chemistry, and foreign languages?

These are complex matters about which professionals will disagree. These topics are inserting themselves increasingly insistently not only into the faculty workroom or the research seminar but also into the everyday, mundane lives of schools. How much technology is appropriate in the kindergarten classroom? "Are standardized tests appropriate ways to measure the abilities of students to solve complex environmental problems? Like it or not, questions like these are facing educators across the globe. The public, used to instant responses on the Internet, seeks reassurance that a rising generation will prepare for the challenges that await it." wrote Dennis Shirley

Requirements for Teacher certification; In most states, candidates for different routes must have at least a bachelor's degree, preferably with a major in the academic subject he or she would like to teach. This education must allow individuals to accelerate their transition to the classroom, as teacher preparation programs for these candidates can be completed in a world of rapidly accelerating technology, understanding how

technologies work, what they do and their potential for benefiting society is critical to a child's future. Technology and coding are the new languages of tomorrow.

Chapter XV Examples of Programs

Providence Public School District Technology Plan Blueprint

The Providence Public School District will be a national leader in educating urban youth.

The Providence Public School District will prepare all students to succeed in the nation's colleges and universities, and in their chosen professions.

Seven Steps to Building School-to-Industry Partnerships

Meeting your match for mentors, internships and expert assistance.

By Kathy Baron

Fourth Industrial Revolution & the Impact on Education

Tom Vander Ark, CEO of Getting Smart

CoSN Consortium for School Networking

Provide current and aspiring education technology leaders for PreK-12

What If the Future of Work Starts with High School? Heather E. McGowan

Why school kids need more exposure to the world of work, Kate Torii, Victoria University

In drive to increase manufacturing workforce, Sikorsky and Teamsters partner to reach high   school students. By Stephen Singer, Hartford Courant

Center on Education and the Workforce – Georgetown University Anthony Carnevale

Since 2008, we have conducted research related to Jobs, Skills, and Equity to better inform students, parents, teachers, and

policymakers about the changing relationship between education and careers.

The CTE Technical Assistance Center, Rexford, NY

The New York State Education Department (NYSED) in carrying out its mission of improving the quality, access, and delivery of CTE through research-based methods and strategies resulting in broader CTE opportunities for all students.

Why You Should Start a School Industry Partnership Initiative by Saul Wagner

National Skills Coalition, Washington, DC

Partnering Up – How industry partnerships can bring work-based learning to scale

ACTE, Baltimore, MD

To provide educational leadership in developing a competitive workforce. ACTE strives to empower educators to deliver high quality CTE programs that ensure all students are positioned for career success.

Asia Society, New York, NY

The work of the Center for Global Education at Asia Society is made possible by our council, members, founding corporate members, supporters, and staff. Learn more about who we are and get involved!

Developing the Young Workforce, Industry & Education Partnerships,

Scotland's Youth Employment Strategy; asks business to be more involved in informing, inspiring and hiring youth talent. Educators and businesses working together as co-investors to create a skilled workforce for Scotland's future.

The Council for Corporate & School Partnerships', New Hampshire

The mission is to identify, create, recognize and support exemplary business and school relationships that improve the student experience in K-12 schools in the United States. To obtain a copy of the Council-developed Guiding Principles for Business and School Partnerships, or to learn more about the Council, its members and work, log on to www.corpschoolpartners.org.

BUSINESS/COMMUNITY PARTNERSHIPS, WALES, WI

To successfully prepare college and career ready students, we fully recognize the importance of leveraging the "It takes a village" approach! Accordingly, the Kettle Moraine School District depends on partnerships and the generous support of parents/guardians, business/industry professionals, and educational and civic organizations to help provide real, rigorous, and relevant learning experiences for our students.

BUSINESS AND EDUCATION PARTNERSHIPS, SPOKNE, WA

It's about creating partnerships between business and education. GSI understands the importance of developing strategic partnerships and works year-round to bring educators and employers together for the benefit of students and businesses, helping our economy and quality of life.

Southwest Technical Education District of Yuma, AZ

At STEDY we recognize the importance of solid educational partnerships. The endeavors of a successful joint technical education district cannot take place without the commitment and involvement of other equally committed organizations.

Education and Business Partnerships, Frederick Country, MD

Network of partnerships of education, business and industry based on a community vision for fostering a quality

workforce through education. Five years later, the school system celebrated the signing of 200 formal business partnerships since the inception of this program.

Industry / Education Partnerships (thejournal.com) October 1, 1998

Mutually beneficial partnerships involving community groups, educators and the business community are flourishing, contributing substantially to better teaching and learning. These range from individual school and district relationships with business and community groups to federal, state and local partnerships involving many universities and a coalition of businesses. Educators are forming partnerships for a variety of reasons. Every alliance has its own needs and objectives and has moved far from supplemental funding and monetary donations. These include assistance in professional growth of staff, sharing of management and organization skills, donation of equipment and materials, technology support, public relations expertise, research and development resources, sharing of curriculum and teaching expertise, among others.

Many examples exist and have been well documented by organizations such as The National Association for Industry-Education Cooperation, (Amherst, NY), The National Alliance of Business (Washington, DC), the National Association of Partners in Education, Inc. (Alexandria, VA) or the Center for Workforce, Preparation, Northeast Industry Education Labor Alliance, Inc. (Springfield, MA) and Quality Education (Washington, DC), to cite just a few:

• Western Governors University (WGU) is a good example of a public-private partnership. The $9 million budget required to launch WGU was raised partly from the participating states ($100,000 from each of 18 states, plus a $3 million grant from Colorado). The majority of the funding comes from AT&T, Microsoft, Novell, IBM, Cisco and others. The sponsoring companies get spaces in the "Smart-Catalog," a Web-based

course directory, and offer corporate training curricula. The degrees are competency-based; students graduate by demonstrating mastery of a particular field, possible job experience or past courses rather than accumulating a certain number of credits. (http://www.wgu.edu)

• New York City's District 6 is one of 225K-12 schools nationwide where students and teachers have access to laptop computers 100% of the time. Through partnerships in their communities with parents and with Microsoft, Toshiba, Compaq, Acer and AT&T, they embrace the concept of "Anytime, Anywhere Learning." (http://www.microsoft.com/ education/k12/aal/)

• The Workers' Compensation Bureau given early 1,800 used PCs to the Lynchburg-Clay School District in Ohio. As of this writing, the 486 machines had network and video cards but still needed additional software and other peripherals, according to business administrators.

• The US West/National Education Association Teacher Network project is training 4,000 teachers in 14 states who will train 40,000 of their colleagues in applying telecommunications in the classroom to enhance student performance. The project will reach over 10% of teachers in the participating states.

• The University of Pennsylvania (Philadelphia) is working with sixth, seventh and eighth grade students from a neighborhood city middle school to teach the nutrition and good business practices, and serving the community with a neighborhood produce market.

Risks and Rewards

Corporate-sponsored internships are ongoing. Educators are given the opportunity to upgrade and update their skills and knowledge working with companies such as Polaroid, Proctor and Gamble,

General Electric, Apple, IBM and many others. Not all partnerships, however, are successful. University officials from California had announced a California Educational Technology Initiative. The plan called for a group of high-technology companies & emdash; Microsoft, Hughes Electronics, GTE and Fujitsu America & emdash; to invest $300 million into the university system's network and technology infrastructure. In exchange for their investments, the companies were promised revenue opportunities from products and services, including software sold to students. The plan has been canceled, though, reportedly due to a lack of agreement on the financial aspects of the negotiation.

Educational improvements are still recognized as the primary goal in developing partnerships. The International Society for Technology in Education (ISTE) found the following elements critical to forging strong, productive partnerships:

• Top Level Leadership - Partnerships seldom succeed in the absence of a visionary school or community leader. In business partnerships, this individual can help identify a core group of leaders who are prepared to embrace a bold mission statement and agree upon the imperative to share risks as well as benefits.

• Grounding in Community Needs - A thorough needs assessment is essential to consensus building; this assessment should address facts as well as the community "mood" (the political, social and economic factors at work among the populations).

• Effective Public Relations – Partnerships must build and maintain support for the efforts. In addition, partners must work to involve the entire community, fully respecting the ideals of inclusiveness, diversity and pluralism.

• Clear Roles and Responsibilities – Precise delineation of roles and responsibilities is essential. Agreement on goals must be followed immediately by a detailed articulation of strategy (who will do what, when and where).

• Strategic Planning - Partners must define goals and measurable outcomes, build a detailed implementation plan, and develop a process to monitor and evaluate progress. Establishing a dynamic and flexible management structure should be a top priority.

• Shared Decision Making and Interagency Ownership - The partnership must benefit all collaborators. Relationships based on trust, open communication and mutual appreciation are critical.

• Appropriate Resources and Technical Assistance - Obtaining necessary resources is often among the most stubborn problems confronting partnerships. While businesses may donate equipment, and parent-teacher groups may raise money, additional efforts to receive it and maintain "donors" deserve and demand high level commitment.

• Patience, Vigilance and Increased Involvement - Successful business/community partnerships involve a long-term sustained commitment from the collaborators.

Partnerships, hopefully, shall continue and flourish. However, some well-meaning industry reformers who seek to make education "cost-effective" or "different" forget education is an entitlement for all, not just a few. Businesses should do more than provide grants and financial support. Educators are looking for "true partners" that can lead to benefits for each partner and address the needs of the educational community as well as each partner's concerns, desires and capabilities.

"Growth Mindset Thinking = Innovation and Creativity"

Norman Halls

Norman Halls is with Norhals Group, LLC, a provider of workplace solutions with offices in Southwick, MA. Formerly in manufacturing and taught college courses in industrial psychology.   He can be reached at halls@norhalsgroup.com